DOG TRAINING THE NATURAL WAY

BY MARTIN GARNER

RoseDog Books
PITTSBURGH, PENNSYLVANIA 15222

The contents of this work including, but not limited to, the accuracy of events, people, and places depicted; opinions expressed; permission to use previously published materials included; and any advice given or actions advocated are solely the responsibility of the author, who assumes all liability for said work and indemnifies the publisher against any claims stemming from publication of the work.

All Rights Reserved
Copyright © 2009 by Martin Garner
No part of this book may be reproduced or transmitted
in any form or by any means, electronic or mechanical,
including photocopying, recording, or by any information
storage and retrieval system without permission in
writing from the author.

ISBN: 978-1-4349-9486-8

Printed in the United States of America

First Printing

For information or to order additional books, please write:
RoseDog Books
701 Smithfield St.
Pittsburgh, PA 15222
U.S.A.
1-800-834-1803
www.rosedogbookstore.com

Contents

Introduction 1

Basic Principles of Dog Psychology 3

    In this first chapter you'll discover the basic tools Dog Psychologists use to communicate with and lead dogs, allowing you to accomplish life-long, lasting results with a minimum of fuss and time. We also discuss the importance of a dogs diet...

The views noted regarding diet are not those of a dog health professional and you may therefore wish to consult an appropriate professional before acting on such information...

Model Behaviour 13

    With the base tools of Dog Psychology at your disposal you'll decide on some simple rules, boundaries and limitations you'd like your dog(s) to observe and help you start putting this into practice.

Mental & Physical Workouts 19

    During this chapter we discuss the importance and practice of walking your dog (the misconceptions and the truths). We will also discuss the importance of mental stimulation and how to cater to the "need of the breed"!

Essential Commands 25

    This final chapter is about teaching your dog(s) essential commands to keep you and your dog safe, building on your core knowledge and practice of Dog Psychology...

Appendix 1: Daily Exercise Requirements 29

Introduction

How would you like a stress-free, simple way to train your dog and achieve immediate results?

I know that seems an outrageous claim - but it's true.

This course is so simple you will likely find it difficult to believe that such an approach will work, let alone help you achieve life-long, lasting results. However, if you patiently and persistently follow the approaches and techniques I will share with you then your success is but a matter of time. In fact, of the numerous people I've taught these approaches and techniques too all have successfully trained their dogs and gone on to lead a happier and more fulfilling life together.

No matter what you've tried before, it's time for you to succeed the easy way - the natural way...

This book is laid out in four simple chapters - four key lessons that will help guide you with ease to success and a better life together with your dog(s). I've taken great care and consideration to ensure that the approaches and techniques presented don't overwhelm you and that anyone can easily learn and understand what I will share with you in this book.

You hold in your hands a book that has the potential to change your life for ever...

To your success and a better life together,

Martin Garner

Basic Principles of Dog Psychology

If there is one thing that dogs desire it is strong leadership - and the love, affection (and most importantly) balance that leader brings.

Leaders are determined by their scent, body language and actions/reactions - in that order. Why in that order? Because a dog processes the world first through use of their nose (their sense of smell is the strongest of their senses), then they experience their world through their eyes (and dogs are a master of body language, unlike ourselves), and then by what they hear. If a dog perceives a "stable strength" they perceive a leader. However, it's important to note that dogs can also determine when we are unstable yet strong, stable and weak and unstable and weak - these are the characteristics of a follower. If a dog perceives another "follower" joining the pack (or they're joining our pack - leader and leadership lacking) they are wondrous souls as they do their utmost to fill that void and help everyone achieve a balanced and harmonious life.

The problem with allowing a dog to lead a human comes in a variety of forms, some environmental, some due to a lack of social skills, etc. So, in truth, the kindest thing we humans can offer our canine companions is leadership...

Dog Leadership

Being a dogs leader is both a mind set and a way of being. In order to be deemed a leader in the eyes of our dogs you must do a few simple things:

Be calm and assertive

Create clear rules, boundaries and limitations for your dog(s) - and make sure your dog(s) observe them

Protect your dog(s), and be accepted for protecting them in the eyes of your dog(s)

Provide for your dog(s) physical, mental, and emotional needs and general wellbeing.[1]

---

[1] This means; providing their food and water, giving affection, providing mental problems for them to solve to keep them mentally challenged, taking them for walks to burn off their pent-up energy and maintaining their overall physical condition, etc.

Your dog(s) should be calm, relaxed and submissive at all times - the role of a follower!

Protection of your dog is a seemingly complex part of dog leadership, but basically you need to make sure your dog is safe from other dogs as much as possible dangers in the environment. For example; ice under foot or broken glass on the pavement. I have a rule of thumb with other dogs; when in doubt if your dog will be safe, don't allow your dog to interact with the other dog(s) - or remove your dog from interacting. Prevention is a simple affair; have your dog sit down and manoeuvre between your dog and the other(s). Utilise corrections on the other dog(s) to create some protective space around yourself and your dog. If the other dog attempts to manoeuvre around you, move in a circular motion and counter with corrections!

Corrections

Corrections should not be confused with punishment. The purpose of a correction is to disrupt the unwanted behaviour and/or inform the dog(s) that they have broken a rule, boundary or limitation set by the ourselves. Corrections need to take into consideration two factors to be effective:

- **Timing** - Correct too late and the correction will be misunderstood or possibly misinterpreted as correcting the wrong act.
- **Intensity** - The intensity of the correction, either verbal or physical, must match the intensity of the dogs mind to effectively catch their attention and thus inform them that the act is undesired or they are breaking a rule, boundary or limitation.

Corrections come in two forms; verbal or physical, verbal being the least severe and physical being the most severe. In turn each type of correction can have different levels of intensity:

- **Verbal** - These corrections are usually a sound or a word to both disrupt and inform the dog(s) of the behaviours unacceptable nature. The word is never the dogs name as this is often reserved for recall and other niceties. The soft tone is the least severe correction and the most desirable if we must correct any behaviour, followed by a moderate tone and finally a loud tone.[2]
- **Physical** - These corrections are touches that are intended to momentarily disrupt the minds attention from its present act to the touch or inform that a rule, boundary or limitation has been breeched and that it is not permitted by the leader. Touches vary both in the three more obvious levels of touch (soft, moderate and hard)[3] as well as by position on the body (neck or hind quarters). It is also possible, as the most severe form of physical correction to send the dog into a submissive position on its back where it must completely relax in this posture before the correction can be considered accepted and the dog allowed back up. Touches can be just that, touches, or we can be more "naturalistic" by using our hand in a rough claw formation to simulate a bite as wolves do in the wild to correct wayward pack members.

2   Bare in mind that the tone used must never become frustrated or angry as at this point we either tend to intensify the behaviour as we're perceived to be unstable ourselves and thus unable to lead, let alone correct, in that moment or get ignored for the same reason. Frustration and anger serves the human in venting these emotions but immediately displaces us from a position of leadership. However, if this mistake is made it is important to forgive ourselves and merely move on...

3   When we say touch we do not mean we hit, there is a difference. It should also be noted that hard does not mean hit either, it means firm and assertive. It may help to play out a conversation in our minds when we offer such corrections to assist ourselves in projecting the assertiveness of our correction.

Praise

So, whilst we know how to correct, the question now arises; how do we praise desired behaviour? Most people tend to regard treats as a means of praise, but honestly, there is a no-calorie alternative you always have to hand - **affection**! Affection can take two forms; the first is being proud of our dogs behaviour. Remember how dogs are a veritable master of body language? Well, your proudness of their behaviour shows in your body language - a language dogs are masterful at comprehending. It's also worth noting that this form of affection rarely disrupts the dog from being in a flow of good behaviour as the other two forms of affection may well do! The second means of affection is one we understand well; that loving cuddle, stroke or verbal praise...

Baring all this in mind I'm going to give you an example of how leadership occurs:

You're out on your daily walk with your dog(s) when you encounter another dog and their owner. The owner has their dog on a flexi lead, the dog darting about in front of them. Now, if this is happening we can safely assume the owner doesn't have a lot of control over their dog in that moment but being the leader means we are going to take charge and protect your dog(s), making sure they observe the "no barking and growling at others" rule we've decided to establish. So lets take you through the process step-by-step:

1. Before the other owner and his "darting dog" are on top of you and your dog(s), we locate a space we can move into that's safely out of reach of the oncoming dog and owner allowing them to move by unimpeded.
2. Moving to that chosen space you then get your dog(s) to sit. Why sit? Simply put, it's harder to be more excited from the sitting position (even more so if lying down, so let them if they so choose and it's safe to do so).
3. Remain clam yet assertive, ensuring you haven't tensed on the lead(s), and keep yourself between the oncoming dog and owner so as to block and protect your dog(s).
4. Well, aren't you behaving well - but is/are your dog(s)? The moment your dog(s) begin to perk up their ears or wag their tail they're starting to get excited, go ahead and offer a correction if this happens. Misbehaved again hey? Go ahead and repeat step 4 every time this happens, ensuring you remain calm and assertive and continue to block the other dog and owner.
5. Once the other dog and owner have moved on by ensure that your dogs are clam and relaxed, then we start walking again. No need to say anything to your dog(s), once they're calm and relaxed we just head off to continue the walk again.

There, leadership in action - pretty simple by all accounts once you get to grips with it!

The nut-shell is; praise the behaviour you want and correct unwanted behaviour...

Sometimes, you can offer a correction only for your dog to go back to their undesirable behaviour - again, and again, and again. The trick here is not only to correct the unwanted behaviour, but to then redirect the dogs "impulses" through a desirable activity.

With the basic tools of Dog Psychology and Leadership now at your disposal the next chapter will build upon this core knowledge and show you how to bring about simple yet wondrous results that will not only enrich your lives together but keep you safe, balanced and blissfully content. But before we do lets just briefly conclude this chapter with a quick note regarding a dogs diet and commercial dog foods...

Dogs & Diet

Oftentimes one of the most misunderstood concepts regarding dogs, a dogs diet is one of great importance. So what we shall briefly conclude this session with is a simple look at the misconceptions and truths of dog foods:

Some Dog Food Misconceptions Include:

- All dogs foods are much of a muchness...

Half true; the fact that many dog foods are "much of a muchness" is owing to the fact that most dog foods are essentially garbage. Not to worry, there are commercial dog food out there that you can trust - such as Burns!

- If a dog food says it's: "100% nutritionally complete and balanced" it must be true.

It's a lie; This is a technical legal claim based on information studies using isolated nutrients as opposed to whole foods. Of forty known nutrients ensuring a food contains appropriate amounts of a dozen or so of these nutrients hardly assures the food is "complete"...

- Dog foods would NEVER contain ingredients harmful to my dog!

False; there are as many as 28 ingredients that can be in dog food that are lethal to dogs and detrimental to their health if they survive, 15 that are unnecessary but harmless in moderation and 25 that are nutritionally useless but harmless to dogs. That's 68 dog food ingredients your dog might literally die for!

A poor diet can eventually cause a variety of ills (that are often attributed to old age in dogs) as the cumulative effect of a poor diet and it's potential contents take symptomatic effect. These may include:

Kidney Cancer
Bladder Cancer
Stomach Cancer
Spleen Cancer
Leukaemia
Liver Dysfunction
Major Organ Failure

Immune System Collapse
Severe Allergic Reactions
Birth Defects
Blindness
Chronic Diarrhoea
Hair Loss
Behavioural Problems - Including Increased Aggressiveness!

If that weren't enough, it should be noted that a poor diet can cause your dog(s) to die 8 - 10 years earlier than they should through natural causes. For more information on dog food misconceptions and truths I would advise you visit www.thedogfoodconspiracy.com

Personally I feed my 4 year old Labrador Retriever (Sarah) home-cooked meals. To ensure the correct nutritional balance I base all her meals upon the equal proportions rule set forth by John Burns in his companies "A Guide to Natural Health Care", p.36. In doing so I feel I'm able to ensure the quality of ingredients that goes into my dogs diet and therefore not only ensure she has a nutritionally balanced meal - but one that will keep her healthy and happy for years to come.

What's more, the variety of meals I've developed for her stave off potential boredom at mealtimes and are comparatively quite cost effective.

Model Behaviour

During the previous chapter you discovered how to take the reigns of leadership, so now you need to decide on all the rules, boundaries and limitations you'd like your dog(s) to observe and ensure that every one you need to know knows and stick to the rules, boundaries and limitations you've set. You may need to offer corrections if a rule means that a certain behaviour previously gotten away with/allowed is now deemed unacceptable, but just as the previous chapters example, keep at it and the consistent corrections will be sufficient for your dog(s) to eventually get the idea. You should also note that if your dog(s) behave in a way you'd like them to you should praise or treat them to reinforce the desired behaviour.

AGAIN - Praise the behaviour you want and correct unwanted behaviour

Rules These are the actions and/or reactions to other people/dogs, things and circumstances that we have noted (in particular) are either allowed or forbidden. When a dog acts in accordance with a rule they are being good and hence praiseworthy.

Boundaries Boundaries define areas off limit to the dog(s), either permanently or until given permission to enter by the leader...

Limitations These are provisos that are attached to a rule. A limitation dictates just how far a dog may go with a defined rule, providing clarity to that rule. An example of this would be; play with toys when given (Rule), but do not play so roughly that the toy is destroyed in any shape or form (limitation).

So, lets begin to determine the rules, boundaries and limitations you wish to set...

Below is a list of the recommended rules, boundaries and limitations - along with the reason(s) for each. But please note that as your relationship matures and flourishes between you and your dog(s) you may wish to change some of what follows. If you wish to alter or add to the list please do so:

Rule #1   Obey the leader at all times!
   This is a core rule that should never change as it belies the core principles of Dog Psychology, the very foundations of you and your dogs relationship. This is the golden rule that overwrites all rules. When in doubt, do as the leader instructs rather that rely on events and rules of the past. With this rule we ask our dog(s) to live in the moment and trust in our strength and stability - our leadership.

Rule #2   No barking, charging at or jumping (excitedly or not) at other people or dogs, unless invited to do so...
   With this rule and proviso we inform our dog(s) to show some manners. I'm sure you'd rather you or your dog weren't mauled and traumatised by another dog (large or small) simply because the dog lacked the base understanding of polite behaviour. So we simply ask the same of our dog(s). Ideally our dogs should greet with a calm (not over-excited) wag of the tail, nose sniffing in the direction and head bowed low in respect, moving toward us with a slow and respectful gait.

We should also be able to ask our dogs to desist the greeting at ours or another's instruction/signal, and respect their right not to interact if they so choose...

Rule #3   Cease an action at the behest of other human or dog, obeying the humans orders above that of a dogs.
   Another rule (and stipulation) to establish consideration towards all others. We ask our dog(s) to defer to the human above the dog(s) as we would respect the opposing rules of another leader and their pack. The other leader commands the opposing pack encountered and thus etiquette demands we defer to their instruction towards members of that pack over the followers.

Rule #4   NEVER guard the home or garden!
   This is a preventative rule, intended to prevent the potential development of territorial aggression (at worst) and immediately prevent barking and growling at passers-by and visitors knocking at our door. Again, it's some base manners...

Rule #5 NEVER guard another person or item

Another preventative measure, intended to prevent possessive aggression and dominance aggression (to an extent). As a leader we protect and own all items at all times. Therefore, this shouldn't be a complex rule to establish. It's also worth noting that simply because you gave a dog an item doesn't mean it's his from thereon out - you simply give him permission to have until you choose to take back (or if edible, eaten).

Rule #6 No entering or exiting a building before the leader.

This is a rule that's wise to implement (during a dogs training at least) as it relies upon a base dog psychology principle of "leader first" and helps to affirm your status with your dog(s). This rule also ensures a dogs safety to some extent!

Rule #7 No entering or exiting a vehicle without permission of the leader.

Just as **Rule #6**, this rule not only helps us assert our role as leader in the mind of our dog(s), but (again) more importantly ensures a degree of safety for ourselves and our dogs - particularly given the changes in environment a vehicle can engender when exiting the vehicle!

So, are there any rules you'd like to add or remove?

Boundary #1 An 'instructed distance' must be observed when doors are opened or answered, unless otherwise informed.

This boundary demanded is to allow ourselves the freedom to pass through the doorway and/or tend to the visitor without being impeded by our dog(s) being on top of us. The boundary still enables the dog to welcome others into our homes (or businesses) or be with us, but without the consistent fighting to do what we desire.

So, are there any more boundaries you can think of that may be useful?

So, how do you educate your dog(s) to adhere these rules, boundaries and limitations? Quite simply you assert your leadership and praise the desired behaviour whilst correcting the unwanted behaviour. Patience and persistence will ultimately reward you with the rules, boundaries and limitations being understood and practiced by your dog(s)...

REMEMBER - You're the LEADER...honest!

Mental & Physical Workouts

Whilst studying the basic principles of dog psychology we noted that part of being a dogs leader means providing for their physical, mental, and emotional needs and general wellbeing. Most of what we have learnt and applied thus far (completed during Essential Commands) has met the emotional needs for our dogs and catered for their general wellbeing. Leadership, ensures we protect, provide and guide enabling all concerned to enjoy a balanced and harmonious life together. But what I shall teach you here are the tools to meet your dogs physical and mental needs.

We shall begin this session by discussing and guiding you through the nature of physical exercise before moving on to discuss and guide you through the psychological needs. In each part we shall also explore how to provide for the "need of the breed".

Walking the Dog: A Physical Workout

It may seem obvious to say this, but when walking your dog (on a lead or not) you should ensure you lead the dog - not the other way around. But next time you're out take a look around you. Based on what you know about dog psychology thus far what do you see? More often than not the people around you seemingly lack the awareness that their dogs are leading them and the dogs can be seen leading their apparent and unaware owners; either by pulling on the lead, darting too and fro in front of them, etc...

Regardless of breed or size, all dogs need to be exercised. A walk is one of those physical workouts that plays to the instinctual aspects of dogs and thus is a prime means of meeting the physical needs for them. It's also worth noting that physical exercise helps release pent-up energy and contributes to a dogs sense of balance and overall wellbeing.

Bare In Mind - Don't exercise you dog and behavioural problems eventually ensue!

So, here's one technique for exercising your dog(s) presented step-by-step:

1. When getting ready to walk your dog(s), call the dog(s) to you, do not go to the dog(s) to put the lead(s) on.
2. After the dog(s) comes to you make him/her/them sit calmly before snapping on the lead(s) or slipping on the collar(s) and leads.[4]
3. Take your dog(s) to the front door and open the door, making the dog(s) sit quietly whilst not allowing the dog(s) to bolt out the door.[5] The dog(s) needs to see, you are the one deciding when it's time to leave.
4. As soon as your dog(s) is/are sitting quietly at the exit, it's time to leave. Be sure you exit the house before the dog(s), even if it's just a step beforehand.

[4] Retractable leashes are not recommended, as they provide less control.
[5] If this happens simply bring your dog(s) back and try again!

Whilst out walking (observing any appropriate rules you determined in the previous chapter) ensure you're calm and relaxed and that there is no tension in your arm or the lead or collar as this "weakness" is communicated to the dog(s) - and we know full-well what this will mean, bye-bye leadership! All you need to do is lead your dog(s) with them at your side or behind (but never in front without permission of the leader), but always paying attention to you for what to do next and where they are going. Now, given the lead has come into play at this point I shall briefly provide you a means for correcting with this tool before we conclude our step-by-step guide for exercising/walking the dog...

Correcting with the lead: to correct with the lead we simply match the intensity of our dogs act with a sideways tug. This tug momentarily throws our dog off-balance and informs them something is wrong. Used in conjunction with a verbal correction the purpose of the tug quickly becomes apparent to our dog(s).

5. Returning to your home (or chosen destination) we get our dog(s) to act calmly and wait whilst we open the door (giving us space as we so choose), not allowing the dog(s) to bolt inside the door.[5]
6. As soon as your dog(s) is/are quiet you enter the house first, followed by your dog(s).

7. Ensuring the dog(s) calm and relaxed we remove the lead(s) and collar(s).

Provided you followed each step you'll not only have walked your dog(s) with a minimum of fuss, but you'll also have shown them you lead them outside of the home as much as inside of the home - whilst providing for their physical needs.

Failure to correct with the lead?

This is quite a common problem, don't fret as I'll now explain how you can compensate when you fail to correct with the lead. Simply put, when a dog misbehaves (and we fail to correct with the lead) all we need do is calmly and quietly bring the dog back to the spot where things went wrong. Back at this spot we get our dogs to sit and calm themselves whilst we do likewise to regain our composure (leader is calm and assertive). Once we've collected our composure and we're ready to try again all we need simply do is begin walking without saying a word. We move off in silence to mitigate as much excitement as possible from the dog and his/her mindset (a follower is calm and submissive).

Our message is simple; you're not getting where you want that way!

To discover just how much exercise your dog needs daily, refer to the back of this book.

When you've successfully applied the techniques above for meeting the physical needs of your dog(s) (and mastered some of the essential commands we shall discuss later) you may be left wondering if there is an alternate way - one that requires no lead. Fortunately the answer is a resounding YES! In the absence of the lead a dog must respond to certain commands and hand gestures (mainly 'recall' and 'heel') at any given time. If your dog doesn't act accordingly you should really keep your dog on lead and continue this training until mastered for both your own and your dogs safety. However, assuming you dog is aptly responsive all you need do is ensure your dog is in constant motion to burn off their daily pent-up energy and hence meet their physical needs - it's as simple as that. Other practical forms of exercise for you and your dog(s) include; swimming, jogging and/or running...

The Need of the Breed: Providing a Mental Workout

Although a physical workout partially stimulates a dog mentally it is woefully insufficient to expend their mental stimulation needs. Indeed, as much as a walk provides release for pent-up physical energy, maintaining physical health and staving off some boredom it is the metal workout that is also needed to achieve complete balance, harmony and general wellbeing for a dog.

Just as with physical exercise, a lack of mental stimulation leads to boredom, and if left unchecked and provided for, may well be the catalyst for behavioural problems in one form or another!

There are activates that are universally enjoyed by all dogs that provide the necessary mental stimulation that derives from their common "dog" ancestry, such as; a treat ball or dog pyramid...

Treat Ball - Let you dogs work how to get the tasty treats out.
Dog Pyramid - Put treats into the Dog Pyramid and let the dog work and swing the treats out. The Dog Pyramid stays in its place and self-rights after being knocked over to release a treat.

Catering to your dogs Breed

Each breed of dog has been bred over the years to fulfil a specific purpose. When our dogs are left to there own devices this breeding forms part of their preferred activities to keep themselves amused. If our dogs are unable to fulfil their needs in line with their breed they defer to a more primitive "dog-orientated" activity to fulfil their needs.

For instance; a Labrador Retriever was originally bred to retrieve fishing nets in the icy waters off the coast of Newfoundland. Over the years this role changed to the retrieval of game in the roaming English countryside from the 19th century to the modern day. Nevertheless, this breeds purpose has remained unchanged since the 17th century. Therefore, it's little wonder that these gentle and loving dogs take naturally to games of fetch with a tennis ball.

Providing for the mental wellbeing of your dog truthfully begins with a comprehensive understanding of their origins. Hence; Border collies can be taught to herd their toys or washing into a low-lying basket to mentally stimulate them. A Bichon Frise thoroughly enjoys a good game of hide and seek - sniffing out their owners, family and friends. Why not visit http://www.dogbreedinfo.com/purebred.htm to gain a better understanding of your furry friend and see if you can think of a creative game to play that caters to the need of the breed.

Essential Commands

During this final chapter you'll learn fundamental commands to keep you and your dog safe, and as previously mentioned, ultimately enable you and your dog(s) to enjoy walks off-lead. So, lets get too it shall we? The commands you will learn here are; sit, stay, leave, up, down and recall. All commands are presented with a step-by-step guide for successfully accomplishing each one...

Ensure you have a lead and collar attached before commencing the exercises below...

Sit

1. Command your dog(s) to sit.[6]
2. Praise your dog once they are sitting.

[6] If this fails do not say anything, rather gently place your hand on their rear and gently guide them into the seated position.

Alternatively...

1. Hold a treat in your hand(s) near the dogs nose (in your clasped fist) and let them get the scent of the tasty morsel on offer.
2. Once your dogs are calm and relaxed, yet still focused on the treat, move you hand(s) towards your dog(s).[7]
3. Praise once in the seated position.

[7] Use the word "sit" as your dog begins to sit, however if your dog(s) simply move backwards just try again...

Stay

1. Command your dog to sit.
2. Once in a "sit position" praise as usual and ensure your dog(s) is/are calm and relaxed.
3. Issue the command "stay" and calmly turn around and walk away.[8]

4. Return to your dog(s) after a brief moment or two and praise.

[8] If your dog sneaks up behind you turn, offer a correction and take them back to their original position, repeating steps 1 and 2 and try again.

Leave

   1. Give your dog something.
   2. After a minute or two command your dog(s) to leave.[9]

[9] If the dog(s) leave the item immediately praise the dog(s). However, if they do not gently tease the item from the dogs mouth(s) and as they release re-issue the command "leave". Wait until the dog(s) is/are clam and relaxed while you have the item them re-affirm the command by saying "leave" one last time - try the exercise again until you have a success!

Up, Down & Entering a Car

   1. Bring your dog(s) to the car (or stairs in you home) and have them sit.

Car Continuation...

   2. Issue the up command.[10]
   3. Get your dog(s) to sit in the car for a moment or two, ensuring they're calm and relaxed before proceeding to the next step.
   4. Issue the down command.[11]

[10] If the dog obeys award with praise, if not lift the dog into the car - and try again once the remainder of the exercise is complete.

[11] If the dog obeys award with praise, if not nudge the dog until it begins to perform the act and as they exit the vehicle issue the "down" command again - repeat exercise until you're successful!

Stairs Continuation...

   2. Once calm and relaxed issue a stay command.
   3. Walk up the stairs and say "up".[12]
   4. Get your dog(s) to sit in for a moment or two, ensuring they're calm and relaxed before proceeding to the next step.
   5. Issue the stay command and walk back down the stairs.[13]
   6. Command your dog with "down".[14]

[12] If the dogs respond aptly immediately praise this behaviour. If your dog(s) ignore their name(s) however walk up to them and calmly bring them to the position you were waiting for them to come to you at - try the exercise again until you have a success!

[13] If your dog sneaks up behind you turn, offer a correction and take them back to their original position, repeating this step.

[14] If the dogs return immediately praise this behaviour. If your dog(s) ignore their name(s) however walk up to them and calmly bring them to the position you were waiting for them to come to you at - try the exercise again until you have a success!

Once you feel your dog(s) is/are ready try this exercise without going up and down the stairs first yourself...

Recall

1. Command your dog to sit.
2. Once in a "sit position" praise as usual and ensure your dog(s) is/are calm and relaxed.
3. Issue the command "stay" and calmly turn around and walk away.[15]
4. Call your dogs name(s).[16]

[15] If your dog sneaks up behind you turn, offer a correction and take them back to their original position, repeating steps 1 and 2 and try again.

[16] If the dogs return immediately praise this behaviour. If your dog(s) ignore their name(s) however walk up to them and calmly bring them to the position you were waiting for them to come to you at - try the exercise again until you have a success!

It's always best to end an exercise with a success rather than a partial success or failure, so when you decide to try these exercise with your dog it's important you make the time for mistakes as they learn. It's also more beneficial to try these exercise after you've exercised your dog(s) as they'll have less energy to contest your wishes with.

That's it - Congratulations and all the best, I believe in you!

Until next we meet,

Martin Garner

Appendix 1
Daily Exercise Requirements

What follows is a general rule of thumb for daily exercise requirements for particular pure breeds. To determine the exercise needs of a hybrid; subtract the needs of the least active of the two pure breeds from the most active's noted needs. Then simply add this difference to the least active of the two pure breeds, of your hybrid, to determine a general rule of thumb in his or her particular case.

Breed	Daily Exercise Needs
Beagle	2 - 3 hrs
Bichon Frise	1 - 1½ hrs
Border Collie	2 - 3 hrs
Border Terrier	2 hrs
Boxer	2 hrs
Cocker Spaniel	2 - 2½ hrs
Dalmatian	2 - 2½ hrs
Deerhound	2 hrs
German Shepherd	2 - 3 hrs
Golden Retriever	2 - 3 hrs
Greyhound	1 - 1½ hrs
Irish Setter	2 - 2½ hrs
Labrador Retriever	2 - 3 hrs
Lhasa Apso	40 mins - 1 hr
Mastiff	1 - 1½ hrs
Newfoundland	1 - 1½ hrs
Old English Sheepdog	2 hrs
Papillon	40 mins - 1 hr
Pointer	2 - 2½ hrs
Poodle (Miniature)	1 - 1½ hrs
Poodle (Standard)	2 hrs
Rhodesian Ridgeback	1½ - 2 hrs
Rottweiler	2 - 3 hrs
Staffordshire Bull Terrier	1 - 2 hrs
Siberian Husky	4 - 6 hrs
Weimaraner	2 - 2½ hrs
Whippet	1 - 1½ hrs
Yorkshire Terrier	40 mins - 1 hr

It should be noted that puppies (dogs aged 10 weeks - 3 years) can require an additional hours exercise to fulfil their physical needs. Furthermore, you should bare in mind to build up any dogs physical condition gradually to prevent any injuries or illnesses.

Occasionally you can cut short the noted daily exercise requirements and perform what I like to refer to as the maintenance walk. A maintenance walk, for most breeds, should be a mere hour - certain low activity breeds (such as Yorkshire Terriers) may get by on 30 minutes. However, it should be noted that it only takes one or two consecutive maintenance walks before your dog begins to try and find alternative means to release his or her pent-up energy. Ideally try to save your maintenance walks for harsh weather or illness and injuries...